D1533336

DAY'S WORK

Dai Lee
,9 April 91.
Green River

DAY'S WORK

DAVID LEE

COPPER CANYON PRESS / PORT TOWNSEND

SwC
811.54
Lee
10.95

SWEETWATER COUNTY LIBRARY SYSTEM
SWEETWATER COUNTY LIBRARY
GREEN RIVER, WY

Grateful acknowledgement is made to the following periodicals and presses which first published some of these poems: *Midwest Quarterly, Willow Springs, Spoon River Quarterly, 5 a.m., The West 13th Street Rag, Tailwind, Weber Studies, Crab Creek Review, Elkhorn Review, Plainsong, Ellipses, Rattlesnake Mountain Broadsides,* Brooding Heron Press and Copper Canyon Press.

"Castrating Pigs" received the *Elkhorn Review* Poetry Prize, 1989. *Day's Work* won first prize, Book Length Poetry, Utah Arts Council Creative Writing Competition, 1988, and the Publication Prize, Utah Arts Council Creative Writing Competition, 1989.

AUTHOR'S ACKNOWLEDGEMENTS : The author wishes to thank the National Endowment for the Arts for a fellowship grant which stimulated the writing of this book and Southern Utah State College for a sabbatical leave during which most of these poems were written. Special thanks to Tree and Sam for faith; to Jims B. and H., G, Clewell, and Jerry for encouragement; once again to the A team: Royce and Mark Barton, Elaine Paulson and Ron Johnson; to Jan for standing by me. The Ellis Britton poems are for Chant and Ruth with love.

Publication of this book was supported by the Utah Arts Council and the National Endowment for the Arts. Copper Canyon Press is in residence with Centrum at Fort Worden State Park.

Copyright © 1990 by David Lee
ISBN 1-55659-027-X
Library of Congress Catalog Number 89-81836

The type is Sabon, set by The Typeworks.
Book design by Tree Swenson.

COPPER CANYON PRESS
P.O. Box 271, Port Townsend, WA 98368

FOR JON AND JODEE, WITH LOVE

y también para el jefe Wayne y doña Arva Cloward,
cuentista maestro y anfitrión esmermada:
salud, amor, dinero y bastante tiempo para gustarlos

Contents

DAY'S WORK

Morning

Hello?
Hey, Dave?
John? What time is it?
Did I wake you up, Dave?
No. I had to get up and answer
the phone. John?
Dave, you sed you'd come hep me
if I needed some one day and I do
come on over.
What time is it, John?
Put on your tennis shoes and
run that mile you do
I'll have breakfast ready
in a half hour when you get here
we'll fix dinner and supper too
leave Jan a note
it isn't no use to wake her up
tell her you'll be home
this afternoon or evening
it's some things I gotta get done.
John?
I'll see you in a few minutes
we'll eat and get started.
          John?
Bye.
          John? It's
five o'clock in the morning.
                    John?

After an All-Night Farrow

The thin moon
burns silver
in henlight.

Then gold lace
falls like dew
on the sheetiron roof.

Now sun sprays
the pasture
and the duroc boar's shoulders
with fire.

Rooster: flap your wings!
Scratch up
a breakfast song
for these eight
newborn children.

Sonnet on the Sun, Rising

Cold. Last night a skiff
of snow. So I
got up five o'clock, made
a fire. Watched the sky
                        unbuild.
I mean, I'm
drinking coffee
                by myself. Shivering.
And I'm cold.
        So it's time, you
        wonderful son
of a bitch. Get on up.
                        I'm ready.
                                Now.

Phone Call

Hello.

Hello, Mr. Williamson? This is David Lee, I live in Paragonah. During my morning run I passed by your stockpens west of Paragonah and I saw that one of your cows, the black white-face, I think, seems to have calved during the night. I think around sunrise, the calf was still steaming, at least I think so. But the cow seems to be in some trouble, I think her uterus has prolapsed and she probably needs some help. I was running and I didn't stop and walk over to see, instead I turned around and came back to call and let you know so you can go out and see if she needs help.

Who's this? Is this church business?

No, no. Wallace, I'm the guy who runs out by your stockpens every morning. You wave at me. Today I ran early and saw that you've got a cow in trouble. She's an angus-hereford cross. She's calved and her vagina has protruded. You ought to go out and check on her as soon as you can.

Is this about selling Amway?

Listen
:goddammit, this morning
in your west pen
the black balley dropped her calf
and her ass is out

down to her knees.
She needs help.

Oh goddam
it's that two year old heifer
I didn't know she was that close
I gotta go.
Look mister whoever you are
you call back
take and give my wife your name
I owe you
but I cain't talk now
I gotta go
but I sure thank you
I'll make it up to you
someday somehow
                    Bye

January: Unloading Feed

Godamitey it's cold
that dam wind don't help a thing
I think I may be loosing
another finger and two toes
and that ain't the coldest part

I heard spit freezes
about fifty below
so hold it in I don't want no holes
in the side the barn
when it's that cold
pee stacks up
my daddy sed oncet
he's in Montana with a womern
had to chop her loost
from the ground

hurry up and get that other sack
out the truck
let's go in and warm up
before the rest of us freezes
and falls off

Fence Repair

What's the matter with you today
sed John you and Jan fighting?
Oh no I said it's not that
it's a letter I got that's bothering me.
Must be from the govament
or the insurance, I can understand that.
No John, it's not them this time
it's from a friend.
Did he die or summin?
you ain't sed a decent word all morning
I might as well be working by myself
and let you set on the nailkeg
unrolling barbwore

Oh dammit, John,
it's just a letter that pissed me off,
I said. It's from a writer who saw something I wrote
about coyotes killing sheep
and he wrote saying that never happens.
He sez what? sez John.
He said there's no documented evidence
that a coyote ever killed a sheep
unless it was rabid, I said.
And he said my story was a lie
and should never have been written.
He's a writer? sez John
What does he write about?

Oh he writes novels, I said.
Books about cowboys and Indians
and the California mountains

He sez that sed John
did he? You know
most chickens I known of
is layers and most folks
I known is liars
and most of them don't know the different
but that don't get in the way
of their opinions.
It was a preacher
got his first call
to come to our town back home
his first sermon that everbody
showed up to hear
was how all people is good
it ain't no such of a thing
as a bad person

he wasn't in town half a year
before Travis Newberry
knocked up his daughter in the eighth grade
and he was twenty-four by then.
He'd started preaching late
after giving up on farming
and owning a grocery story
must of been too late
he run out of words after about a year
we had to elect him to office
to give him something to do.
First thing he voted no taxes
and no pay raises to schoolteachers
so they all known he'd be a good one
mebbe governor some day

had to move him out
of the parsonage and into a house
where he had to pay rent
like real people
so they found him a place
out on the end of town
where they could be alone
with that pregnant girl
they took out of school.
It was skunks out there
a mama and four babies
and his wife and that girl
sez oh they're purdy
let them alone, we like them
so he did
by the time she had her baby
they'd killed all their chickens,
the Easter ducks and the cats
it was mice and skunks
running all over that place
they couldn't live there no more
so he run for state office

they sent that girl
off to Christian school
we never heard of her again
and tried to raise the baby boy
but couldn't do that neither.
He got elected
on the campaign of no taxes
and close down the schools
cause he blamed it all
on Travis Newberry hanging around
the jr high parking lot
and moved to the state capitol
to live and before

they could rent that house again
they had to set out traps
for two months and rat poison
sed they got twenty-four skunks
but nobody counted the mice
it was awful
took a year for the smells
to go off and it wasn't no hippies
back then to rent it to
they had to wait it out

so he run for Warshington office
six years later
and put the boy in the orphanage
up for adoption
he might of been a scandal
but he didn't get elected
they made him a judge instead
after that and he's rich
still there and being so famous
he don't pay no rent
the state give him a house
and a car and a maid

but that still don't mean he known one dam thing
about people or skunks or mice
or preaching or farming or
running a grocery story.
I seen it with my own eyes
a coyote running through
a herd of sheep and killed nine lambs
just to do it
and we set up five nights
in our pickups waiting for him
until he come back
and he killed four more

before we shot him
and that's nothing to what
Allen Dalley out to Summit lost
that one year when they say
coyotes got half his lamb crop
that's just a bunch of bullshit
because he done one thing
don't mean he knows nothing
about anothern
and if he doesn't know
what he's talking about
you tell him to just keep his mouth closed
or run for office
that's what it's there for
so why don't you forget about it
and you can forget him too for now
let's get to work
cause all this is real
not something in a book
and has to be got done for sure
not just by thinking about it
and if you don't get that frown put in a drawer
this is gone be a long day of work

Faith Tittle

HEBREWS 11:1–3

John, I said, have you
ever spayed a gilt?
What'd you say? sez John
I said castrated a female pig
it's called spaying.
I known that
I known what spading is
I just cain't figger out
why you asking

It was this Ag teacher
back home I remember
who wanted to be a vet sed John
he didn't make it neither
so he did the next best
he liked to try
all them fancy operations
he's good on ruptures
and worms and even
untwisted a horse's gut oncet
I heard and cow's eyes
he castarated a bunch of chickens
made them capers he sez
sed they'd grow fancy feathers
and get fat and sell
for a lot of money
but they all died first
and he cut some girl pigs

spaded them up
most of them died too
nobody known if it was his fault
the ones that lived
was just like barrows
ate and got fat and never come in
It was this one womern
in town we called Faith Tittle
back then cause it was her name
call her Judy now I heard
that was real fat
she couldn't lose no weight
if she tried so she taken and went
to the doctor and he give her
thyroid pills and diets
and examinations
finally he sez she has to have
a hystericalectomy for womern
they gone take all her female parts out
and then mebbe she wouldn't be so fat
Doctor told her, Faith Tittle
it's something inside I cain't see
some substance I just hope
I can get rid of for you
and then you'll be better off

Faith Tittle wasn't sure
she'd do that cause that doctor
he'd been a Babtist
medical missionary, he played
piano music in his office
and she's a Cambellite
she couldn't trust him for sure
so she went down to anothern
to see what he thought
and he played band music
in his office and was a Methodist

so when he sed yas
she ought to have it all took out
she wasn't married anyway
and was arredy over thirty
wasn't doing her no good
she figgered he'd believe anything
and probley change his mind
about it at the same time
so she sed she wanted to go off
by herself and work it out
where there wasn't no music
playing because that one doctor
he sed we better take out
the whole works and she's afraid
without that she's about as good
as dead and was it worth it

She went to her kinfolk
Leonard Tittle, he's a Cambellite preacher
I don't know what kin he was
he'd been a algebrar teacher
at a high school but his breath
was too bad, the kids couldn't stand it
when he leant over to help
with their homework
they'd of rather failt than had him hep
so he had to finally find
something else to do
that he could be good at mebbe
so he took to preaching
at the Lorenzo ChurchofChrist
she sed she didn't know what to do
he told her some Methodists
and Babtists wasn't all bad
they might not go to heaven
but they could do operations
on earth okay and he'd pray

it'd probley work out

so she done it
they cut her open
both doctors was there at the same time
hauled off a wheelbarrow load
of stuff come out of her they sed
that operation wasn't no more
than sewed back up
news was all over town
from the nurses and doctors and wifes
they found knots of flesh
and hair and a set of teeth
inside her womb growing there
they didn't know how long
and lumps the size of a cantalope
down to a golfball
took it all out and thrown it
in the trashcan
except the hair and teeth they sed
it got put in a jar and sent off
to Warshington to see what it was

She's ruint
all over town they's talking about it
her business was everbody's
and down in the flats
they's scared to death of her
say her name out loud
their eyes swelt up like a coffeecup
they sez she been with the devil
you could pull out a wad of doghair
they'd have a spasm
thinking it might be her hairball
I'd of love to had a set
of falseteeth back then
but I never

Faith Tittle had to leave
it wasn't nothing there
for her no more
she went before the Cambellite church
and asked to be prayed for
with the rest of the sick and afflicted
then she changed her name to Judy
they sed and left
dunno whar she went
it don't matter, Leonard Tittle
stood up in the churchhouse
sed all things wake to the good
for those which love the lord
and he's her kinfolk
so I spoze she come out okay
wherever she went
to start over again

but no
I never done one, have you?
What? I said.
Spaded no girlpig
what are you talking about?
I just cain't see no advantage
if the boar stays in his pen
where he's posta be
until it's time to turn him in
they eat the same as any hog
either way just the same
so what's the different
why take a chanct
if you ain't sure
what you're doing?

Building Pigpens

meanest man ever
was Ellis Britton
I known of him for years
before I known who he was
I went to school with his boy Melvin
we called him Swamprat
he's half cross-eyed couldn't help it
he got killed in the war jumping out airplanes in Franct
he flown all over the world in the army
before he got killed they sed
is it a longboard over there anywheres?
we can put a longboard on the bottom rail
to stop digging out mebbe
so onct he was driving along in his car
he seen this man building a pigpen
he's doing the front fence
and it was this level he was using
to get it straight because
it was beside his house
you could see it from the road
he wanted it to look nice he sez
Ellis Britton he stopped his car
rolt down his winder
and sez what in hell are you doing?
you don't use no goddam level to build
no pigpen you stop that
that man he waved Ellis Britton drove off
that night taken and come back

SWEETWATER COUNTY LIBRARY SYSTEM
SWEETWATER COUNTY LIBRARY
GREEN RIVER, WY

he torn that pigpen apart
right to the ground with a crowbar
sez he couldn't stand it no more
to put on no airs that way
hand me them nails in the sack
them sixteen pennys

he raised hogs for awhile
couldn't stay in the business
he killed his boar one day
this sow was posta be in
he put the boar to her but she
wasn't ready that boar he
didn't want to wait round
got excited cut her side open
with his tuskies
god it made Ellis Britton mad
he run in his house got his gun
come back he shot that boar
in the head but it was a twenty-two
the boar was old had a thick bone
it never killed him at first
he run off squolling
Ellis Britton he chased him down
shot up a whole shirtpocket
full of bullets killing that boar
cut this board off where I marked it
with the nail right there see?
he killed two other pigs
and shot four more other ones
that never died
when the boar went down
he busted the twenty-two acrost his head
and he'd give it to his boy
for a Christmas present
it wasn't even his

he was deer hunting this time
and it was this horse
he'd borrowed from his wife's brother
so he shot this deer
tried to load it on the horse
they's a long ways out
that horse didn't want to carry that deer
he hadn't done that before
so Ellis Britton tried to load him
but he shied
goddam you cut the wrong mark
I sed the one I marked with the nail
where's that board?
you done ruint it find me anothern
so he give it three tries
then he got his gun
shot that horse and walked home
his wife had to call her brother
and tell him so he could go get
his saddle off the dead horse
if he wanted it
how about that one over there
the long one will it work?

had to put him in jail onct
it was this boy rode his motorsickle
at night Ellis Britton he was sleeping
he rode it by his house on the road
out front riding round these blocks
he went by a few times
woken Ellis Britton up he couldn't
go back to sleep so he got up
went out in his shed and got his rope
he tied it to these two trees
where it went acrost the road so
here come this boy
it's not long enough

is it one any longer out there?
look in that pile over there
he hit that rope right on his shoulders
busted out both collarbones
they sez if it'd been a inch higher
it'd of tore his head off
and broke his neck
soon as he hit Ellis Britton run out
in the street he taken out his knife
and cut holes in both motorsickle tores
he went back in his house
never even called the ambulance
neighbors had to when they heard that boy
screaming Ellis Britton went to bed
bring that one over here
I think it'll be long enough
they arrested him and put him in jail
so next morning
Charley Baker's daughter she was a idiot
her tongue stuck out her mouth all day
slobbered down the front her dress
she brought these breakfast
it was scrambled eggs with applesauce
on top of it she'd fixed
and slud it in his cell
she set down to watch him eat it
like she always did
you couldn't stand to eat with her
setting there slobbering at you
so most prisoners they'd just slud it back
she'd eat it right in front of them
with her fingers
it was puke all over that jailhouse
after breakfast some days
she could remember and find the ketchup
can you cut this one right?
follow the mark right there

don't cut it half in two this time
Ellis Britton he set right down in front of her
on the other side the bars
he eat the whole thing with his hands
her setting there watching
when he's done he used his fingers
sopped up the rest
he slud the plate back so she picked it up
and looked at it then she
turnt it up and licked this one spot
Ellis Britton he jumped up
he reached his arm through the bars
grapt that plate he sez
goddam is it some more on there?
that's mine you cain't have it
Charley Baker's daughter she hollered
like hell she run off
wouldn't bring him nothing else
they let him go that afternoon

so he got this job as a conductor
and ticket taker on the railroad
he dam near ruint that whole run
it was to whar it was a line
ever Thursday and Saturday
to take the greyhound bus
nobody would ride the train
see I knew you could do it
if you'd pay attention
that education has to be
worth something you'd think
they sez some folks would go on
to the next town twelve mile away
and ride the bus back or hitch
just so they wouldn't have to have
Ellis Britton help them get off the train
and find their suitcase

he was so mean
how come you just standing there?
find anothern board
we here to work
not just set round wasting time
so then it was this other time he taken and

Coyote Dope

You can make this bait
I heard about from somewhere
all this meat and blood rotted
in a jar that stinks
they can smell and come
if they in the mood for it

is that water boiling?
put them sagebrushes in it
we'll boil the oil off the traps
get the smell gone
when you lift it out the pot
don't touch it with your hands
use them pliers and a hook

I don't use no bait
they too smart for it
somebody turnt a jar over of it
in my pickup oncet
you cain't get that smell away
I had to trade it off finally
put the trap
under a bush where
they done been before
and sprinkle coyote piss on it

that's purdy hard to get
cept in a magazine

that costs a lot of money
so dog piss or turds work too
piss is better
on the bushes where they smell it
come up and cockt their leg
to piss on top of it
saying they live here now
they get its leg in the trap
that's how you catch them

it can be embarrassing
getting dog piss
if people come up and see
you getting it
have to foller the dog
around with a coffee cup
for a couple of days
to catch enough to work
he don't do it on demand

okay it's boiling
get it out and put it
in the tow sack
we'll get that sonofabitch

The Tree

Ho Dave, John yelled
let's go buy us some pigs on partners
make some money
with this 400 dollars I got.
What, John? I said
where'd you get 400 dollars
did you kill somebody or did
LaVerne win the Publisher's
Clearing House Sweepstakes finally?
Do you want to get some pigs
or not? sed John and I said
John I don't have any money
I can't buy any pigs right now.
Okay I'll loan you half
on not too much innarest
and you can pay me back
we'll split feed costs sed John
come on let's go

where did you get 400 dollars? I said again
If it's any of your business
I sued myself and won sed John
I said what?
John sez that's a fact
and here's the money to prove it
he put his hand in his pocket
when he pulled it out

all I saw was green wings
fluttering in the afternoon

It was on account of a aspen tree
John sed and I didn't say anything
we was up on the mountain
getting wood when me and LaVerne
seen this big dead aspen tree
standing so I sed
I'm getting that one,
LaVerne sez no you're not
it's against the law to cut down
a standing tree alive or dead
I told her that tree couldn't read
it wouldn't know no better
I drove up beside it and got out my saw

I cut a wedge that would of choked
a dinosaur out of it on the down side
and the wind was blowing north
where I wanted it to fall
I taken and cut downwards
on the up side just right
that tree was gone fall
whar I wanted it to
I'd chop it up and load it
I had the truck up close ready
the radio on so I could listen
to the stockmarket on the 12:30 news
it all looked about perfect to me
I finished the cut and
that goddam big sonofabitch
fell exactly backwards
against the wind
I see it leaning toward my truck
I yelled no goddammit the other way
not that way

it wasn't listening
that tree fell right on down
acrost the hood of my truck
busted my windshield out
and a side winder, mashed the cab
buckled the hood up almost in two
knocked the battrey off its ledge
whar it's dangling in the motor well
and bent the radio antenna
where it wouldn't work
I still don't know how much pigs went for
in Omaha, Nebraska on that day
LaVerne stood there and sez
oh no, oh no, oh no

What did you do, then, John? I said
Wasn't nothing I could do
I'd done watched all that was gone
happen, now I had to go to work
show was over and the radio
wouldn't play no more
not even music so I cut up the tree
and loaded it in the back
I figgered it was mine by now for sure
I earned it so then
I had to get the battrey
wored back up whar it would hold
and I went to see if it'd crunk
it did and the radiator wasn't ruint
I told LaVerne get in
we started driving home

I wasn't back on the blacktop
more than two miles here comes this law
with his redlight flashing
I sed uh oh and LaVerne sez
you better think of something fast

you gone get a big ticket
they'll take your chain saw away too
I sez like hell they will
I's scairt I pulled over
that law got out his car
walked up to my pickup and leant on it
sez pardon me mister
but did you know your winder
was bursted out? I wanted to say
did you have to go to college
to learn to be a officer of law or
did you come by it natural?
he'd arredy sed bursted
I known he's educated
so I sed yassir I do
and I want to file charges on it

He sez what? LaVerne sez what?
I sez yessir it was this way
I was driving along
minding my own buiness
on this public road
on a Sunday it was this man
drove by me with a load of hogs
in his truck, passed me and
slowed down right in front of me
made me hit my brakes
or I'd of run into him
that law sez both of you
hit the windshield and bursted it out?
I sez nosir that ain't how it was
we's right up behind him
one of them hogs in his truck squolt
when he seen us and he taken
climbt up them stockracks
jumped out that truck
right on my hood smashed through

28

my windshield into the front seat
busted out the side winder
getting out it like to of
scairt us to death for sure

that law stood up straight he sez
was it a man in a red and white
pickup? I sed yas, a Ford
I think he sez with stock racks
sort of like yours? yas
sort of I sed, he sed they open different
I think but they're orange like yours
I sed yas I think that's a fact
he sez did you happen to notice
if one side of his truck was dented up any?
I sed oh yas it looked like itus
mashed in on the off side
like somebody'd backed up on him
at a livestock auction at the loading chute
or something, I's hoping he wouldn't
walk around my truck
to the other side he sed
did you happen to see his license number?

LaVerne had her brains
plugged in that day not me
I wouldn't of known what to say then
she sed officer I seen the first part
it was a ABJ license plate for sure
oh it was so awful I cain't believe it
she taken and put her face down
in her lap like she's crying
that law was shook up he sez
she okay? I sed
I was on my way to the hospital
right now I just cain't be too sure
he sez you foller me

I'll give you the police escort
he jumped in his car
turnt on his red light and siren
pult out and led us to town
to the hospital

We had to go in the emergency room
and wait, he come with us
sed can I ast a few more questions?
LaVerne sez oh officer we in shock
I don't see how we can talk now
it's all so terrible and awful
he sed yasmaam I can see that
and don't you worry
I known who the man who done this
to you is and I'm gone get him
for you don't you think about it any
we gone make him pay a fine
can you just gimme your name
and address? I couldn't think
that tree might as well of
mashed my head in it wouldn't work
the only name I could think of
to given him was Richard R. Nixton
and if he'd of ast for my driver's license
I was dead right there
but LaVerne sez LaVerne Sims
before I could say a word
Box 162 and that was her daughter
Peggy's and Warren's box number
and that law sez how you spell that
I sed L-A-V-E-R-N-E and he wrote
it down in his book but it come out
L period Verne and he wrote the rest
I never sed a word
he sez I'm gone take care of this
for you personally I can promise

you that and he left

We set there for a hour waiting
and two doctors come up to help us
we sed we's just company
visiting a emergency case
that was arredy there
we didn't want to leave
in case that law would come back
see us and track us down
finally he didn't and we went home

About a week later here comes
a official letter from the law sed
dear John Simms we have a eyewitness
account of how you was irresponsible
with your hogs and one jumped out
and bursted L. Verne Sims's winder
at Box 162 of Cedar City, Utah
caused personal and property damage
resulting in bodily injury
and you're liable if you
don't get your insurance company
to pay for this we gone arrest you
with a bench warrant
signed Steve Johnston, officer of the law

I said what did you do then, John
and John sed
I taken and sent that letter
to my insurance sez I didn't know
one dam thing about any of this
I didn't know what to do
they sed they's gone sue me
for a million dollars if I didn't
do summin so what am I posta do now?
three days later I got a call

from Pocatello, Idaho the head office
man sez what's this all about?
I sez I dunno your honor
I'm just a farmer I don't know nothing
about the law or the insurance
or the goverment except taxes and driver's license
so he ast me to tell in my own words
my side of the story
I told him *if* a hog jumped out
my pickup what can I do about it
that hog's got a mind of his own
I cain't tell him what to do
or who to go live with
and what's somebody doing
follering me that clost anyway
ain't there a law about that?
besides who's gone pay me
for my hog that would of been worth
a hundred dollars at least
if he's big enough to bust out
a winder like that
and now he's gone I think
they stoled him and I ought to
get something out of it
bet they done eat it
besides my insurance going up
I didn't think it was my fault

insurance man sez whoa now
when I told him I's ready to cancel
I couldn't afford no raise in price
especially after I done lost
my best brood sow in that wreck
he sez way he sees it
it's a act of god
couldn't nobody of stopped it
and he gone offer a 500 dollar

settlement if they won't take it to court
and if L. Verne Sims sez that's okay
then they won't raise my insurance
and do I know this L. Verne Sims
is he any kin of mine?
I sez no I don't know no
L. Verne Sims or other man by that name
he ain't no blood relation of mine
or otherwise so he sed
will that satisfy you? I sed
I don't spoze I'll ever be happy
about losing a pig that way
but I cain't have no insurance going up
so if that's the best I can do
it's bettern I'm usually treated
he understood and said he's real sorry
but he'd do what he could

After that Peggy brought us the letter
mailed to her mailbox
from the insurance and we sed
we'd accept the 500 dollars
and let it go at that
wouldn't press no charges and
in a week here the check was
and a sheet of paper
to go down and get a bid to have
the damage fix they'd pay for that too

I taken the truck to Parkland
he sez John I'm gone bump this up
I can iron this out and get you
a used windshield for about 300 dollars
I'm gone bid this for 500
won't nobody know the different
and I'll take and give you
a good deal when you're ready

for a new car later on
I sed that's fine write her up
he bid it 500 dollars
I sent it in
another week I got another
500 dollars so I went down to A-1 Glass
got me a new windshield
for a hundred dollars and
a radio antenna and got my tractor
power take off fixed and the feeder
on my bailer and two new tores
and I still got 400 dollars
for us to spend on pigs
for partners

John, I said, your hood's
not that mashed up, how'd
you get it fixed?

Man at Parkland's he calls me up
sez John brang your truck down today
I got you a pointment
we'll get her fix up good for you
I sed nothankyou I believe
I can live with it like it is
he sed goddam you it's a law
you got to have that truck fix
I wrote a bid and the insurance
he given you the money for it
he sent me a copy of the letter
now you bring that truck in
like it sez or I'll call the police
I sed you can go fuck yourself
I ain't doing one goddam thing
to, for, with, on or under you
and if you call the law
you tell him about jacking that bid up

it's my word against yours
I can holler at least as loud
as you can he sez
you'll hear from my lawyer about this
I sed that's fine
tell him don't write me
write my lawyer and I give him
your name and hung up.

What? I said. So then
sed John I call Peggy and Warren
sez yall come out this afternoon
to see us and bring the kids
LaVerne wants to see them and
we'll watch T.V. and talk
they can play outside
so they did and when they come
I told them kids now look
I done spent all week
getting that truck hood over there
bent up like I need it
I'd done took it off and had it
laying on the ground
so yall stay away from it, hear?
we went in
five minutes later I heard them
jumping on it I waited ten more
minutes and went out the door
them kids took off to the corral
they'd done the job
I called Warren can you help me
a minute? he come out
we lifted it on the truck
they'd stomped it out almost flat
we didn't even have to monkey
the holes to get the screws to fit
it latched first time

I banged out the cab
with a hammer, and it's almost
good as new it'll last
till I trade it in a hundred thousand miles
or so

so are you inarrested or not?
What? I said interested in what?
in buying hogs on partners
I got 400 dollars left to spent
and I sed I'll loan you half
we'll make us some money
so what kind we gone get?
And I said yes, John, I'm interested
How about durocs?
Judaspriest no sed John
you cain't build a fencet strong enough
to hold them let's get black listed ones.
But they get rhinitis, John
and don't grow
Well we damsure ain't getting
Chestnut Whites that'll sunburn
all summer and shake their fat off
freezing all winter I want
dark ones or spotted or listed.
How about Yorkshire?
That's okay if it ain't white or red.
Well, John, now listen, we. . . .

Feeding

If I didn't love that boar so much
I think I'd kill him.
Why, John? I said. He's not that old.
For his hide, sed John
look at all them spots
you tell me that wouldn't make
no good rug or billfold
hanging on the wall
with the hair on
them spots all sticking out
except I don't know how

How what? I said
Tan that hide soft with the hair on
cain't you pay attention?
give him some more
he's still hungry
I seen him holt a whole cantalope
in his mouth at oncet
he can eat moren that
I think it takes a special juice
or summin I know if you rub the hide
with his brains after you bust
his head open with a axe
the hair'll fall off and the skin go soft
but I cain't do it the other way
besides if I go to all that trouble
I'm having scramble eggs on them

I'll hang the hide on the shed
and buy a billfold
I don't need one that bad anyway

back home Rufus Garner
was the undertaker and he known
the secret of how to do it
he made all his belts and stuff
and his wife name Edna Mae
about the purdiest purse of horsehide
she'd wear on her arm
to the funerals and picture show
she told everbody Rufus could do anything
with a dead body except
make it talk or have supper
he could fix them up no matter
how bad they was busted
or eat up with the disease

oh my god she'd say
you should of seen that one
they turnt him on his face
when they operated and all his blood
run to its head and it swole up
its face turnt blue when it died
we gone have to use the suction
get all that out and it's jelly by now
it'll just set in the sink
till we through and then
it won't warsh down
I'll have to get it out with a soup dipper
if you had a cup of coffee
in your hand when she talked like that
you'd have to set it down somewhere
you couldn't finish it no more
you'd lost the taste by then

this other one
you should of seen she'd say
it was like you taken a razor
cut it round and round
whar he went thru the windshield
his eyes wide like this
staring at you whar Rufus
couldn't find his eyelids to pull them shut
till he got all the swolen out
and its face to go back down
from the size of a basketball
the cuts pult shut and sealt
but that casket will be open
so help me god you can come see
what it looks like right now
Rufus got tored of all that blood
up his arms he's taking a rest
so come on it ain't nobody there

the town idiot beside the Bakers
and Fosters was name Jasper
back then that's what we called him
he'd come in to see the dead bodies
if they wasn't tore all apart too bad
he couldn't take that either
till Rufus was done with them
but he liked to see them on the table
he wouldn't touch them
but only stand and look
so oncet one had his stomach muscles
wad up like they do sometimes
oncet in awhile they'll blow out
like they been holding their breath
or their legs'll move
this time it set up straight
Rufus hadn't sewed its mouth shut
so it hung open too

like it was getting ready to talk
Jasper didn't wait
he turnt round fell
right into the closet
where they kept all the funeral clothes
they put on dead people
got tangled up in hangers
started hollering and jerking
like them episcoleptics do
they had to call the sheriff to help
get him out of there

so Rufus got his start in Wyoming
right after he went to funeral school
in a little town somewhere
he run the undertaking
and a taxidermist shop
with a wall between
but the same working room in the back
behind that was where they lived
and the storage room
they's so poor at first
they didn't have no furniture
to set on like chairs
it was two sawhorses and a used door
for a table to eat off
with all the deerheads he's fixing
on the wall watching them
Edna Mae sed they slept in the caskets
when they went to bed at night
and if it was a big one left over
they could sleep together
when their baby got borned
it was a baby coffin they had
for a crib
for the first two years it was alive
until it got used up

but it never known no better
they had to get by

Rufus sed his best one was there
that he almost couldn't get fix
it was this trapper's wife that died
in the winter in January
too much snow and too cold
to bring her in for the funeral
he laid her out straight in the bed
opened the winder while he left
to run his traplines
she's froze when he got back
he couldn't sleep with her
in that bed and it wasn't nowhere else
to put her in the house
he had to store hides in the attic
so the bears wouldn't smell them
and wake up in their holes
come out after them early
he taken her outside
stood her up in the woodshed
till the weather turnt
whar he could bring her down

so when it did he did
took her to the doctor first
so everbody'd know he didn't kill her
she died of the pneumonia
doctor looked her over to see and
sed so for a fact
then he took her to Rufus
to get her ready

Rufus sed he never seen such
a sight as she was
he didn't know what to do

her face was about two foot long
chin hung down on her chest
both jawbones out of its socket
he thought she's the ugliest womern
he even seen till they showed him
her picture what she's posta look like
he sed what in the hell happened
how'd her mouth get that far
down under her nose?
that trapper sed I be dam
I never noticed I been with her
so long till right now
she'd been dead about two months

ever day that trapper he'd go out
whar she was in the shed
to cut wood for the fire
he'd have to do it mostly at night
working in the day by hisself
he broke off the nail
in the rafter of the shed he hung
his lantern on so he could see
he didn't have anothern
it wasn't enough light on the floor
so he taken and prized
her mouth open to where
he could hang the bail of that lantern
behind her front teeth
to hold it up and it worked
he could see to chop that way
but they figgered
when he done it ever night
that lantern thawed her out
her mouth'd start to hang open
a little till he'd finish chopping
take it off and she'd freeze back up
after two months

her face looked like a boilt clam
hanging open but it happened
so slow he never noticed it
sed he hadn't paid a whole lot
of attention to her face in years
Rufus had to go to the carpenter's
and borrow a furniture vice
to squeeze her head shut
broke both jawbones doing it
he sed he learnt a lot
and the box was open at the funeral
they sed she just looked dead
not horsefaced

he could tell me how to
do that hide with the hair on
if I wanted to kill that pig
but I don't
I don't have the money to buy
another boar right now
I better keep him
you don't need no rug anyway
if you want a hogrug
why don't you kill one of yours
instead of wanting mine?
Give him some more feed I said
you trying to starve him to death?
he's just trying to get by too

Fat

I wish I had the trick
to get these hogs to grow
sometimes I wonder
if it's something wrong
with this pen or not

this is the slowest growing
bunch of pigs I ever had
they just won't eat

I had this cousin oncet
name Roy Don Staples by marriage
he wasn't no sexual relation
of mine but he could teach
them pigs a thing

he's 200 pounds
when he's ten years old
watching him eat
was a education in appetite
when he grown up
he's a barber

he cut your hair
he'd sweat and grunt
round you
like he's gone die
of heat stroke

he's so fat he had to hold
his arms straight out
to cut hair
couldn't even cocket
his elbows

it was enough lard
on his belly
you could deep fat fry
a ostrige's neck

when he's fourteen
his mama and daddy
set him up a table
by the pig pens
to show him what he looked like
eating

after the third day
hogs wouldn't come out
of their shed
they so embarrassed

he swallered a avocado seed
choked to death on it
and died when he's twenty-seven back then
took four days
to find eight men willing
to be pallbearers
that casket's so heavy

I even put sugar mash
in their feed
and wormed them twicet
they just won't grow
goddam them

if I didn't have so much money
invested I'd sell them
for shoats and they said
the ropes busted
at the cemetery

his box fell
in the hole
when they's lowering him
they just covered him up
I wasn't there
let's go

mebbe they'll eat
if we won't stand here looking
mama used to say
it ain't polite to watch
fat folks eat anyway
it makes their self conscious
and some might get
the complex from it

Arthritis

FOR KEN AND BOBBIE

Can you come help me a minute?
Take and grab this thing right here,
now put them pliers on it there
and hold, I'll get a clamp on
wait a minute, just hang on
right there, there. Okay
youg'n leggo it's done and I thank you

I cain't grab holt of nothing tight
today my arthritises is bad
and I haven't got no grip
I swallered four aspurns for breakfast
but they ain't working yet
I wisht I had me a copper bracelet
they say helps out when you got it on
or one of them Mexican chinchilla dogs
you can set with it in your lap
and watch T.V. and it keeps
the arthritis away

Ruby Patrick back home had one
she's Kay Stokeses daughter
married this Jack Patrick rancher
he hit oil everwhere he stuck a stick
in the ground just like Kay Stokes done
so she's rich on both side
but she had arthritis anyway
in her fingers and toes I heard

went all over to them specialist doctors
spend a dam backseat full of money
to find out they couldn't do nothing
and then asked old man Cummings
who could take warts off of you
what to do cause he'd know
he sez get you one of them Meskin
dogs without no hair on it that can fit
in a teacup they advertize in *Grit*
and the funny books and set with it
in your lap a hour a day
and it'll be a whole lot better
but it won't never go away
you might as well get a marriage license
to it so she did

I heard she paid a hundred dollars
for that dog and got papers
to prove it was a real one so
when Kay Stokes heard about it
he thrown a fit till his face swole up
like a tomater sez what the hell
goddam good is that thing?
he had half the money in the world
but a hundred dollars for a dog like that
was one too many for him that day
can it hunt? he sez can it swim?
can it bring back a duck or a quail?
that sonofabitch cain't even set up
in the front seat of a pickup
and see out the winder
what possessed you to pay good money
for a little shiteater fycet?
she sed you get out of here right now
it's none of your buiness what I do
and it's not one penny out of your pocket

so you don't have nothing to say about it.
Any penny spent in this town he sed
is a penny that could of been mine
but he went and left anyway
he never did like that dog
but that was okay
that dog never had no love
for him either

she'd set on the furniture
in her living room with that dog
on her leg and if anybody come in
it'd commence to growl and shake
all over, its lip would come up
its eyes'd bug out like grapes
on a mustang vine
that dog known in its heart
it could whup anything alive
that come in or around its house
or the car if it was in it
you could set there and talk to her
for a hour or shell peas all morning
that dog'd never take its eyes off you
or quit snarling, it didn't like nobody
except her and that included her husband
but she sed it did help her arthritis
and she liked it so there you go

Then these sorry poor people
come to town in a whole carload
it must of been a dozen of them it seemed
we figgered they traveled from one town
to anothern looking for handouts
after they left
nobody got a for sure count
on all them kids

but it didn't seem no way
he could of got the back winders
in his car closed
he'd of had to cut off seven arms
and a leg and three heads

they showed up at the churchhouse
Sunday morning and sed
they want to join up, man sez
he wants to address the congergation
sed my kids ain't ate a good meal
in a week now what ya'll
gone do about it, brothers and sisters?
Wasn't nothing they could do
except have a prayer and take up
a collection but they didn't get much
so somebody sez I think it was
Billie Hill we could bring them back
some food this evening
at the prayer meeting so they did

Mrs. Patrick she brung twelve quart jars
of homecanned peaches she was proud of
she won the blue ribbon almost ever year
at the fair and sez I hope you enjoy them
but could I please have the jars back
when you done? she's polite that time
he sez yasmaam whar do I brang them?
she sez address on the jarlabel
so they loaded it all up in his car
and he taken and drove off
didn't even stay for prayer meeting

next morning here he comes
up the street dragging a kid's wagon
nobody known where he got

probley stoled it with all them jars
in it empty none of them even warshed
and knocks on the door
she sed did you eat all that fruit arredy?
when she seen the wagon
on the sidewalk he sez
good godamighteychrist lady
when we eat fruit we eat fruit, by god.
Neighbors seen her
sed her face and jaw went so tight
she could of bit a hole in a crowbar
never sed nothing
went out the door and picked up three jars
in each hand and went in with them
then come back for the rest
he never offered to help her carry them
but when she come back he sez
anybody in there happen to have
a cigarette? she sed
nobody in that house smokes
that I've ever heard of
he sez well that's your buiness
I expect not mine
she sed it certainly is
shut the wooden door when she went in

he set down right by the yard gate
started picking his nose and whistling
like he worked there for them
for a living at their house
waiting, he's a professional
she seen it right then
through the windercurtains
he's gone wait her out till she come
and sed what do you want?
that's how come he had the wagon
to carry more back to where he come from

well he had the wrong lady
just cause she was expensive
lived in a big house
and had a fycet she was still
Kay Stokeses daughter and that dog
had papers to prove who he was
so she let the sun shine on him
all day till the afternoon
she opened the door a crack
he started to get up probley thought
she's gone offer him some lemonade
here come that dog out the door

he sez hey lady your shiteater
he never got to finish
that dog was on him
went around his ankle three times
torn his sock right off his leg
put a swok right up the back his shirt
like a lawnmower run over him
lit in his hair
grapt a mouthful out and about dug
a hole in his head with his back feet
in about a second and a half
GODAMITEY SONOFABITCH he yelled
jumped up and tried to run
but the dog got in his eyes
and scratched his face
he put his foot in that wagon
and it took off the other way
he fell down on the fence
ripped his britches hollering like a elephant
with its tail in a knot
got up and run down the street
that dog chased him a block
bit him on the finger when he swatted

at it running never broke a stride
he's gone
they left the wagon right there
on the sidewalk for a week
where he turnt it over
but he never come back for it
nobody saw them again
so they give it to the school finally

she sed Carlos!
that's what she called that dog
you come right back here in this house
right now, I didn't say
you could go outside
that dog spun round in the street
and went home like a whirlwind
was after him
went through that front door
right between her legs
and she shut it, it was all over
nobody ever heard what she sed
to that dog or about it
she never mentioned it again

but that dog held her arthritis down
for a many a many year
she'd set with it and pet it
in her lap and even Kay Stokes
sed it cut down on the doctor bills
and the aspurns from Bob Collier drug
but he never did say it was worth it
but then he wouldn't
he wouldn't give a inch for nothing

so I wouldn't mind having one
I'd go watch T.V. with it

and let you fix this dam bailer
I cain't figger out why that feeder
don't work and I cain't get this wing nut
unscrewed come help me
don't just stand there looking
I told you my fingers don't work today

Separating Pigs

That one's gone be hard to catch
I can tell you now for a fact
he's one the fastest pigs
I ever seen
we'll have to get him in a corner
there he goes
get that othern, right there

I wisht I could find me a track
and race him
we'd win us some money
but it ain't one around here
State Legislature wouldn't let us
race pigs anymoren bet on horses
if they thought we's enjoying it
we'd still have to catch him first
you cain't grab him
if you don't bent over
goddam there he goes
you'll have to move faster than that
we need old man Benson
to give you running lessons

we's cutting wood
up around the deep sinks back home
on top the Sawmill Road
my brother'd take off the back tire
put on a belt and rig up

the sawblade
one day here come old man Benson
before he got killed in the wreck
to see what we're doing
and tell us we not doing it right
that saw blade slips off
and comes right at him
usually he's crippled
cain't hardly move
this time he seen it like a deer
run off to the side
right in this pond of water
almost drownded before
we could get to him he's so fast
that saw blade
buried itself in a tree truck
four steps from where he was
so deep we couldn't get it out
if he hadn't of moved that fast
we'd of took him down
for cordwood and it's still there
unless somebody cut it down
you couldn't pull it out for money
he was so fast that day

okay here he is
let's get him this time
before he gets away again
head him goddamit head him

Morning Coffeebreak

The difference between now and then
is when I's young
all I wanted to do was run off
and find me a river
or a stocktank with a tree by it
to hang my clothes in
so I could cool off and swim

now I just think about that mountain
and a aspen tree with leaves
that won't hold still to see what color it is
even when the wind don't blow
the bark so white it's cool
in the afternoon when I set down
with my back up to it
watching a chipmunk go down a hole
and one of us goes to sleep
and the other one don't care
whether he dreams about him or not

Machinery

Hand me them pliers sed John
or look in the box and see
if it's some vicegrips in there
I can get a holt on this with
I wish to hell I'd never bought
this dam swoker used
it's give me trouble
from the day it's born to me
I cain't figger why this dam
feeder bar's stuck this way
but if I can turn this one mebbe
OW goddammit that catch level
kicked me on the knee
go get a sledge hammer
hit it with it
no don't
get me a monkey wrench
mebbe that's what I need

I

Robert Milton had the worst luck
with farm machinery
of anybody I ever known
from the beginnings
he should of been something else
besides a farmer I think
he hitched a ride on a manure spreader

when he's a kid about fourteen
the driver thrown it in gear
to where the spindle turnt
give me a screwdriver
is it one up there close?
I got to get this one out here
one of them teeth got him
no not a dam Phillipson head
a real one gimme
the woodenhandle one
whar he's laying down hiding
that spindle spine come up
on his face and torn him open
he lost a eye out of it
never could see out of it again

nope that don't do nothing
that's not it from here
look you climb up and thrown
it in gear and let me see
what it does if it's going in
he never did have any
of his equipment that worked
he'd buy a milking machine
it'd be hook up backwards
splatter milk all over the barn
then when they'd fix it
the bacterias was in the lines
he'd have to tear it all down
and start over
let it off I cain't see nothing here
I'll slide to the other side
see if it's something there
so when he put it back
the pump went out
had to get a new one
then his electricity'd have

one of them power surge
blow it again
shock the cows or something
okay put it in again
they got to where
some dried up and the others
kicked so much he quit
and went to crops
let it off slow
slow I sed cain't you hear?
do it again oncet more
wait a minute stop now
push it in slow and let me
get my head up here
whar I can get a look at it
now do it

2

he had about four or five tractors
in a row none of them any good
he'd have to have two at a time
one to be busted down
grinding the valves or
putting in gaskets or rods throwed
right there you can stop
I think I see something over here
they was all ruint oncet
he had hay had to be cut
so he used a horse-drawn mower
he borrowed from his daddy's place
where it'd been setting out rusted
but the horses wasn't used to it
they hadn't pult it before
only wagons and kids riding
so this pheasant flown up
to whar one reared

the othern went to the side
that mowing machine must of
hit a ditch or a rock
nobody seen it
he sed the last he remembered
was that bird and he
didn't have no shotgun with him

lookie here I be dam
these gears out of whack
they ain't mesh up
no wonder it don't turnt
how'm I gonna get them back now
you got any idears?
can you see it? right here
bend down you cain't see it
if you don't bent over
get me a pry bar of some kind
is it a heavy screwdriver
or a longhandle wrench?
if I can get this one on

so it thrown him out of the seat
down in front of the cutters
the horses kept going
give me it here
I think that'll work
he got caught in the pointed guards
on the cutter bar
drug him half way down that field
see there it went on
now how come it's coming off?
something's loost somewheres
scalped him
cut off a ear and a kneecap
three of his toes
slit him open all the way down

one side before it thrown him out
he was a bloody goddam mess
all over the kitchen when he got back home
crawling all the way
look at this support bar
it's cracked clean through
you sonofabitch

3

now how we gone hold that together
I want you to tell me?
this ain't no classroom
don't stand there studying
with your hands on your hips
pick up a hammer and hit it
see if that'll work
he's the one you might of read about
the goverment loaned him
money to put in one of them pits
in his cowyard to rake the slurry in
so it wouldn't be muddy
on his shoes in the yard
it'd turn into that
methane gas

We got to get this braced somehow
or it'll come right back off
it might throw that whole rotater
off if it does it again
how them cows done it
nobody knows it shouldn't of happened
but they somehow knocked the lid
down into the pit
where it was a open hole
in the corral they couldn't have
so the hired hand

didn't know no better
none of us had saw one of them before
he clumb down in after it
never come out
that gas killed him
before he known it
Robert's boy was there too
he went down after him
it kilt him too that fast
both of them down there dead
you could see them not breathing
his wife called the police
and the sheriff went down
after them with a hankerchief
over his face but it wasn't enough
now there's three of them dead
they had to get a ambulance
and a foretruck there with gasmasks
to get their bodies out
it was in all the newspapers
Life magazine and *Grit* I think
everbody heard about it
it was him and he shouldn't of
tried it because he knew
he didn't have no luck
with machinery
it's got to be welted

4

I can spot it here
then run a bead along here
to holt it agin the wall
where it won't wiggle loost
but I have to get it home for that
how am I gone fix it for now?
is it any bailingwore up there?

it was a call one night
I answered it and my brother sed
hello John
I sed hello how are you?
he sed I'm fine but Robert's not
he's dead
look the seat post
under where I set
I think I wrapped some around there
in case I might need it
brang it here

they sed he died of a heart attackt
about nine a.m. in the morning
and didn't come home for dinner
Irene didn't think
much about it
and then for supper
she got sort of mad
it was bowling night
she went alone
got back home about nine
he wasn't there
yeah that's good.
give me both of them
I'll wire it in two places
where'd I put them pliers?
she called the sheriff
it was a new one the othern's dead
to go look and there he was
by his pickup dead too

after they hauled him off
they went to bring the pickup home
couldn't start it
battrey's down
he played the radio a lot working

I figger when it wouldn't crunk
that was one too many for him
he jumped out to kick it
probley killed him
too much for his heart
he'd seen enough

okay put it in
let's see if it's gone work
there it is
I think that'll hold for now
till tonight or when I can
get it home to my welter
don't you walk up
on that side of it when
it's running though
it might not holt
if that balingwore busts loost
it might slung that whole wheel off
it could kill you
and bust your leg

that's good enough for now
let's go to work
and get this hay cut
before something else
decides to fall apart and bust

Castrating Pigs

I

All right that's the first half
done and through
you want to take a break
go set in the shade a minute?
John sed and I said yes
my back hurt from bending
while I worked the knife
and needle but
my half was done and I got to hold
the pigs while John cut
and gave the shots

you like doing the cutting
don't you? sed John and
I said no John I don't
I didn't say and you know it
but John knows damned well
that I don't like castrating
that it makes me almost
as nervous as pig killing
you want a coldbeer? he sed
I said no John, not till we're through
he sed it won't give you
the shakes just one
I said I'm through cutting
it's your turn anyway

John sed if that's how you want it
I said John that's what we agreed
I'd cut half and you cut half
I've done almost a hundred pigs
it's your turn
but only half of them was boy pigs
John sed and I said yes John
but I earmark the gilts too
and John sed yeah but
you're better at that than I am
and I said no I'm not John
you taught me how to do that
John sed that's how come
I'm a good teacher
and I knew John was
going to try to get me
to cut the rest of his pigs

2

You got any hangnail clippers?
sed John I got one
it's driving me about crazy
to where I don't think
I could hold on to a pencil
or a knife much lest
one of them shot needles
it's so aggervating
ain't it funny how something
that little can stick out
and hurt so much
whar you cain't even concentrate

Chant Lee back home
that run the flower shop
him and John Heller was moving
this stove out of a widder's house

cause she bought a new one
on a Monkey Ward sale catalog
but if they'd put the new one in
for her she could save more
that's what she told the preacher
he calt them on the phone
to do their Christian duty
so when they was wallering it
away from the wall
to unhook it Chant Lee
got it sideways so the ovendoor
come open and then it
tipped upside the frigerator
slamt back shut
he started hollering stand it up
stand it straight up
John Heller set his side down
where the stove was even
but Chant Lee was caught
in the corner he yelled
open the door open the ovendoor
John looked down
it was shut on his pecker
caught in the side
he couldn't even jump
up and down it might of tore off
so he opened it so
it come out but Chant Lee
sed he had to go to the bathroom
see if it was ruptured
or bruised up too bad

he come back in a minute
John Heller was almost bawling
he sed did the stove fall on you
are you hurt? he sed no
Chant Lee sez why you

looking that way then?
he sed all my life I been
about a half inch too short
for anything I wanted to do
I'd give four years off the rest
if I had a pecker long enuf
to get slamt shut in a stovedoor
that's what's the matter
with me so how come
you didn't tell me
you didn't want to cut them pigs?
I thought you wanted to help
when I called you this morning
if you didn't want to help me
you should of sed so
in the first place
I could of got LaVerne or somebody
to come give me a hand
haven't you got no clippers?

3

Last time we done this
my arthritis was so bad
I couldn't hardly hold on
to the tools you remember
I taken and given myself a shot
of that combiotic two times
that day cause my hands
wouldn't work right
my grip was all give out
John I said you did that
when we were cutting that boar
he knocked you down once
and the needle stuck you
and the other time
you sat down on it

where you laid it on the bucket
oh bullshit sed John I never
my hands wouldn't work
and I couldn't put that needle in
whar I wanted it to go
so you gave yourself a shot
in the butt instead I said
no he sed that was a accident
but it wouldn't of happened
if my arthritices hadn't been bad

accidents like that happen
when your hands won't do
what you tell them to
it was this man name Bill Wilkins
I known back then
who was a countant and did taxes
for the expensive people
who needed it so they
wouldn't have to pay the goverment
he had arthritis
almost as bad as mine's acting today
it was a tradgedy
he was showing his wife
this recipe for cooking hotpeppers
he'd learnt from a Mexican
but you had to peel them
so they was doing it drinking beer
it went thru him he had to lose it
he went back to the bathroom
was gone a few minutes
she heard this awful hollering
run back there
he's laying on the floor
his britches down to his knees
hollering holding a towel
on his private self

because of his terrible arthritis
in his hands he couldn't
turn on the water faucet to warsh
he'd unzipped and grapt hisself
with all that hotpepper juice
all over his hands
it come off and scalded him
he was in a awful pain
nobody known what to do
he sed he was about to get
them water blisters all over
it was burnt so bad
she called the hospital
to see what to do
they never heard of it before
given her the number
at the capitol for the poison control
whar they sed you better
get some butter or crisco grease on it
real fast to get the heat out
it worked he's afraid
they was gone have to operate
but they didn't

he didn't want them to find out
and put it in the newspaper
but they must not of heard
he sed it took three quarts
of olive oil to put out the fire
they never did finish cooking
them hotpeppers after that
he sed he lost the taste for them
all because of his arthritis
and I don't think I've got
no aspurn in my truck for mine
this one hand's purdy stiff

I'll have to hold the knife with
you know I didn't get a cold
that whole winter I give myself
them shots of hog medicine
it's got penicillin in it they say
it works

4

John I said are we going
to finish those pigs today or not?
we've got half left to go
yas we gone finish them up today
I haven't got time
to take two days on it
I'll get it done somehow
even if I have to find a way
to keep from hurting my back
bending over that long
with my bursitis
let's look around see if it's a bucket
I can turn over and set on
to do it so I won't hurt myself
because when we keep on like I was
holding them for you to cut
my back's straight
I can do that all day long
it's that benting over hurts me

got to watch it setting down
even then at my age
something can go wrong
if it's not a natural position
Gideon Clark was splitting rings
they cut off one of them popular trees
that the wood's tough on
and hard to split so they brung it

to him and give it for nothing
to burn but he had to split it
he's old too like me
mebbe a little bit older I spoze
so he set down on the round
he'd drive a wedge in
with a four pound hammer
turnt around on it and put
anothern in the other side
most times two wedges
would pop it apart or get it
so he could whop it
with a maul oncet and bust it

this one time he's setting there
hammering this green piece
he hit the wedge and somehow
it went down but then
popped right back up and out
that popular wood snapped together
closed right up on his privates
that was hanging partly down
in the split part
like a vice slamt shut on him

oh my god oh my god below me
he bellered loud as he could
tried to stand
tried to roll tried
to pull hisself out
his family heard him in the house
come out to see what it was
but it was too horrible to look
what do we do? his grandboy sez
who was there being babysit that day
oh my lord I don't know
his grandma sed I never saw

something like this before ever
Ellis Britton lived two doors down
heard him hollering
come down to see what it was
sez go get a axe and cut him off
then he'll be loost
it's a doctor can sew it back on
oh my god below me Gideon yelled

finally that boy seen the wedge
laying on the ground
where it fell when it come out
he got it back in the split
right between Gideon's legs
about two inches away and hit it
with the hammer four times
before he could get it in
far enough for that wood
to come apart so he could get out
he went straight in the house
went to bed and shut the door
wouldn't talk to nobody about it
his wife had to give
that wood to Ellis Britton
he wouldn't split no more of it
Ellis Britton sold it
to the Babtist preacher at half price
he sed so he wouldn't
have to worry about firewood
and could take care
of the sick and afflicted
see if there's a bucket or something
I could use for a cheer
to set on if I have to do this
over there behind that shed
so I don't kill myself
or ruin my back for life

5

John I said if you want me to
I'll stand in the pickup bed
and hold them where
they'll be up high and you
won't have to bend over
would that be better?
oh no sed John that's not
the natural way you do it
where'd you learn a trick
like that from anyway
I never heard of that before
I don't want no hogblood in my truck
and what if you fell
you might bust your head open
it could be dangerous
to do it that way
one them hogs might bite you
on the ankle in there
you'd get tangled up in the stockracks
trying to get loost
it'd get infected and I ain't got
no insurance if you sued me
we cain't do it like that

we have to do it
the way it's always been done
you know bettern that
you try to change a good thing
never know what might happen
my brother he castarated cats
for people back home
to keep from having too many
running all over town
he'd put them in a army boot

like them you're wearing
upside down and lace them shut
where their butt was up
and he could get them worked on
they couldn't get away
or scratch at him

but this one time he was
coming home from work
they seen him and brung a cat
for him to castarate
he's wearing shoes not boots
it was summertime and too hot
so he couldn't do it
like he always did
he taken off his overalls
he's wearing britches under them
working hay so two layers of clothes
kept him from scratching up his legs
and tied a knot in them
where he could put that cat in
all wrapped up in it and
set down straddled on him

when he starting cutting
that cat had a conniption
to get loost of him
he got one out and was about
to start on the othern
that cat finally bit thru
the overalls his britches was thin
on the butt a old pair
he had on for work
that cat chewed him
right on his intersection and
would of held on
he jumped up sed GREAT godamitey

that cat come out
them overalls like he was shot
out a cannonball
they never did catch him
to finish the job
my brother sed never again
would he ever go to work
without his boots on after that
he pulled his britches down
right there to see
if that cat torn his balls open
it's some things you have to
do the right way or not at all
it can be dangerous

6

John I said do you want me
to cut the rest of those pigs for you?
Do I what? John sed
I said, I said . . .
look John sed if you want
to cut them pigs well I won't
stand in your way from it
all I want to know is
why didn't you say so
before I almost got started
I don't mind doing everything
your way all the time
but you at least
ought to let me known
how it is we're gone do it
so I can make plans on it
we got to work together
if we gone get it done don't you think
but if that's what you want

let's get to it
we're wasting time standing here
you can talk about it later
let's get this work done now
while it's still some light
to see by

Edna Mae

Rufus was the town undertaker
and Edna Mae his wife
lived with him in the back
of the funeral home
where they had another door
it opened to Huffman furniture
he run that too
when it wasn't nobody dead to bury.

You could tell when somebody died
in town, here'd come Edna Mae
down the street wearing her gold
high heeled shoes
she always wore to funerals
and her mink stole rain or sun
cold or hot she wore it
we all called it her evening gown
the whole town would know
somebody's dead before we known
who it was when we seen
Edna Mae's gold high heels.

She helped Rufus out
with the funerals and dead bodies
putting on their clothes
pinning on the corsages and

getting them right
her and Rufus was artists they sed
and I spoze so
didn't matter how mashed up
they was them two could get them natural
so they just looked dead
and the coffin lid could be opened
at the churchhouse to see
even Edgar Turner and his head
was half shot off.

You'd go to the cemetery
after the funeral and at the end
of the line was Edna Mae
and the preacher and Rufus
to shake hands and help feel sorry to
all the family and watchers
she's as official as the sheriff

so she died of the cancer finally
everbody wondered how
Rufus'd do it to her and then
without her and how he'd dress her
but when we got to the funeral
there she was in her box
wearing her mink stole
and the preacher sez she'd done
wrote out all the plans
for her funeral
and the sermon and the prayers
and the singers and the songs
and before we could even wonder
about it they had the first song
and if I live to be a hundred
I'll never forget it

them singing *oh them golden slippers*
at her funeral
and everbody who was there'll swear
to this day when they went by
her box at the end
she's smiling.

Still Life: Lightning Above the North Fields

Agreement at variance with itself:
adjustment under tension, as of bow and lyre.
HERACLITUS

Running on the graveled road
joyously. A small rain, like dew,
all afternoon and an owl

lumped in sodden plumage
tangled in the sleep
of russian olives. Clouds rush,

thick redolence of sage, reverberation.
Road clings to the shoes. Memory:
Art Williamson & his bay

gelding near Beryl Junction
a hundred yards from the tunnel
last year. A fieldmouse

scuttles under glistening barbed wire
into shadows of lucerne. Smile,
or the imagination of smile

imagining the scrim of dream
split by a phosphorescent glow,
rumble in the great vault

cry and flutter of wet wings,
"not I, not I" so thin reply.

Hired Hand

You need some help
out to your place for anything?
What John? I sed
It's a man come around
looking for work
here and there he don't charge much
name Norman and he's willing
to work for money

you cain't get no good help
I hired this one college boy
to help me put sheetiron
on my barn roof
that didn't work out
I told him look
I'm gone splain this one time
and did what I wanted him to do
but ever time he walked by
that pile of sheetiron
he'd stand there combing his hair
in the reflection of it
trying to look purdy
all I had out there was me
and them ewes
I couldn't take a chance on it
whatall might be on his mind
I had to work and the ewes

was arredy bred up
I let him go that day

Norman ain't too smart
but he ain't purdy
and don't worry about it
him and a rooster
could stand there and stare
at a line you drawn
in the dirt with your foot
half the morning till you shook him
but if you tell him
what to do and check up on him
he'll get it done
all of us working together
I imagine we can finish it
before wintertime comes
but he can come help out
over to your place too
I suspicion if you need help
but he ain't much conversation
he just understands
whichever you tell him to do
you shouldn't ask him
for anything more than that
that's all you're paying him for

Digging Postholes

was teaching his boy Melvin
how to play some baseball
so he stolt this baseball bat
off the churchhouse softball team
brung it home
he opened up the garage door
a little bit he put these little gravels
down on the ground inside
had Swamprat stand there
ever evening before dark for a week
holding the baseball bat
and the swallers'd come out
they'd see them gravels
flown down to get it
the way they do
so Melvin when they come in
thru the door
he'd see them coming in out of the light
he'd swat at them with that bat
learning to hit baseballs
that's deep enough
I done got a cedarpost
youg'n go head and dig the next one
Ellis Britton he'd whup his ast
if he didn't hit some
ever night you could hear him
hollering boy you
keep you eye on the sonofabitching ball

you swinging like a dam girl
you want me to get you a orningboard?

Melvin he'd bawl
he'd squowl I'm trying goddammit
daddy them bastards won't holt still
Ellis Britton he'd holler
just clost your mouth boy
here comes anothern get ready
where'd that tamping rod go?
so he'd hit a few they's all squashed up
out in front of the garage
here come the cats

Ellis Britton he knew them cats'd
bring him bad luck
if he let them stay around
so he taken and borrowed this pellet gun
from the preacher's boy
made this one daughter of his
set on the porch with the gun
while he heped Swamprat
learn to hit baseballs
and shoot them cats when she seen it
sneaking up on the garage
to get them dead swallers
it was this one she shot at
ripped him a little bit somewhars
that cat couldn't think of nothing to do
but climb a tree
it wasn't no tree out there
just Ellis Britton
he's hollering how'd I ever
get a piss ignorant boy
like you? you done missed anothern
I'm running out of patience boy goddammit
that cat clumb right up him

that one'll be a cornerpost
dig it a little bit deeper okay?
so Ellis Britton
like he got his tit in the wringer
bellers godamitey godamitey
get him off get him off me
Melvin he sez is it one coming daddy
his daughter she commenced
to pumping that pellet gun up
hollering Melvin Melvin
that cat went right up the side his face
torn whole handfulls of hair out his head
he couldn't grab it fast enuf
just hollers get him off
get him OFF me
his daughter yells Melvin Leon
Melvin Leon pumps that gun
Ellis Britton's wife comes out the housedoor
screams Jesus Godamitey Judastpriest
Swamprat runs out the garagedoor
he sez whar whar? Ellis Britton hollers
get him off get him off
that cat about torn his ear in two
he grabbed holt and was hanging on
Ellis Britton's wife she hollers
do summin DO summin
Melvin he sez whar is it whar is it?
his daughter hollers on his head see him
on his head she shoots Ellis Britton
in the shoulder with the pellet gun
Melvin yells I seen him holt still
Ellis Britton's wife hollers help your daddy
HELP your daddy Ellis Britton he yells
goddam what was that?
when that pellet hit him in his shoulder
he turns round Melvin

he hit him in the face
with the baseball bat

the cat ran off and hid
when he fell down
got away

it should be a big cedarpost in the pile
see if you can find one for the corner
so his nose was busted
it broken off half his front teeth
he had them all pult out
got him some storeboughten ones
sez it wasn't worth it to fix them
it costed too much
most was rotten anyways
they had to operate on him
to get that pellet out his shoulder
that cat never did come back

Melvin didn't get picked
for the baseball team that summer
he could hit but he couldn't catch
he had this one eye it was crossed
he couldn't find the ball
up in the air after itus hit
that's a good one bring it over here
they's afraid he'd get his brains knocked out
if it was a flyball hit on his head
they known Ellis Britton
he'd sue the Little League if it did
so they wouldn't let him play no baseball
they couldn't afford it
stick it in and scrape up some dirt
with your foot and I'll get the tamping rod
so then after that he

The Feed Store Salesman

I ain't going to Overbury's feed store
no more if I want to buy something
don't matter what it is
I'll say gimme a little sack
of sixteen penny nails he'll get out
a big sack sez you'll need moren that
a week later I done got
three flat tores and nails strung all over
the back of my pickup
or seed I'll say I want
200 pounds of alfalfa seed or
eight pounds of red potater sets
I come home with the whole
dam back of my truck full
of seed to plant twenty acres of hay
and the front seat running over
of dam rotten taters
probley left over from his garden

Jiggs King held his own
with him oncet I seen
he come in sed I need to buy some rope
he sez how much you need?
oh he sed we gone stake the calf
in the backyard so enuf to go
from him to the fence
mebbe about fifteen feet or twenty
he pulls about fourteen coils

off that spool sez let's make sure
he don't stranglet on the pickets
Jiggs sed wait a minute
till I get that calf moved up
a little closter to the fence
that's moren I can afford
but I cain't think that fast
he would of solt me
the whole spool for my dam calf

Bargains

You ever bought stuff
on a sell and then had to
spent more than it costed
getting it back right
cause it wasn't worth it
trying to save money? sed John
I said yes I have
I bought a hundred pounds
of laundry soap on sale
that we might as well feed
to the pigs for all it's worth
it won't get clothes clean

don't do that sed John
pourn it on the ground
in their mud holes so when
they waller they'll get clean
LaVerne sent me down
to buy her some jar lids for canning
it was some I ain't seen before
on a good buy that day I got
so when she put them on
not a one of them sealt
we got seven jars of sourpickles
seven more of applebutter in the frigerator
to use up before it spoilt
he wouldn't give us our money back
sed all merchandise was as is

he give me another goodbye
I got a whole drawer full
of jarlids won't work worth a dam
if you know anybody needs some

back home Homer McCreary
took and bought him
a toilet paper oil filter
for his car oncet that was gone
save him fifty dollars over
the life of that car
it might have except it thrown
all its rods in six month
gummed up the cam shaft
had to rebuilt the whole engine
toilet paper and slime all over
down in there ruint
Ab Holm the mechanic sed
you might as well of pourt sugar
in with the oil as use one of them
and to save more money
he'd even used that one sided
toiletpaper that goes thu
on your fingers when you use it
so we figgered he deserved it
for being that cheap

I worked the hay combines
when I's younger from Oklahoma
all the way up to Dekota
mebbe even Canada on that one place
I never known how far up we was
so when we finished and come back
I hitched to that dam Amarillo
where I was gone hop a train
from Oklahoma where I worked
back home to save the money

I had 300 dollars I'd made with me
outside town it was a bridge
that went over this river
without no water in it
ain't no water in that part of Texas
that the train'd slow down for
I had everything I owned
except what I's wearing and
the money I'd made in my pocket
in this satchel I had then
that I'd run my belt through
and cinched up so my hands
was free to grab holt of the ladder
when it went by slowed down
with that satchel banging
on my knees when I run
it had to be a slow place

I grapt that ladder
tried to climb up but that satchel
went under and was
on the other side hung up
on the bridge where if
I let go to keep the satchel
I'd fall off into the river
without no water in it and
break my neck in the sandbed
about a hundred feet down
or if I kept on hanging on
I known I'd get tired
fall off under the wheels
get mashed up for something's breakfast
that I hadn't even seen
or cut up in nine pieces

so I held on and pult upwards
hard as I could till my belt busted

satchel fell in the river
probaley floated off when it rained
if it ever did but I's free
clumb on top and rode
while I fixed my belt up
best as I could so my pants
wouldn't fall down

I had to switch trains
at Wichita Falls to get anothern
went where I's going
but the train wasn't stopping
I had to get off however I could
or go to Houston or mebbe El Paso
I couldn't speak Spanish
so I got down on the ladder
ready to jump off outside the trainyard
got my feet moving like I was practicing
running before I hit the ground
then I let go running
fast as I could so I wouldn't fall
all over my face but my belt
busted again or come loost
my pants went down and drug me
right into one of them cholla cactus patches
down around my legs and
some prickley pears too
I had cactus thorns from my knees
to my ast to my elbows
and some in my neck
had to stay in the hospital eight days
took ever penny I had
I mopped floors there
the last three days at night to make up
the rest of the bill
a ticket home from Oklahoma
costed fourteen dollars back then

a whole summer with nothing to show
it didn't even leave a scar

they oughta be a law
against selling cheap stuff
that don't work to save money
cause you loose ever time
I bought them dam sparkplugs
and Japan points they had
out to Overburys that worked
for about a week and that's all
now my swoker won't start
and I run the battrey down crunking
I got forty acres of hay for Keith Guymon
to knock down I sed fore morning
and I got to tune it up and
buy some more new parts
if you'll go get them for me
I done waste more time arredy
today than I'll ever get paid for
so don't buy me no more
cheap things this time
you keep them for yourself
from now on
don't do that to me no more
so if you'll do that then go on
cause I got work to do

Taking a Break

You ever worry about that boy
of yours? sed John about
the kind of kids he's gone run round with?
John I said I worry about my kids
most of the day and all night
and I don't think I'm ready
for you to prime the pump

no I never meant it that way
John sed it ain't no use
to go and get a head start on it
I just wondered who
he's gone grow up and be like
I always heard you's gonna be
like what you grown up round
that and what kind of blood
you got in you
it was a boy back home
come out of good people
his daddy run a grocery story
had a good living
that boy took up with Travis Newberry
before long he's riding motorcycles
all the law known him by name
sure enuf they caught him
busting in to the school
stealing lunch money and then
Ben Edwards hardware store

they known Travis put him up to it
but they couldn't catch him
sent that boy to the reform school
he's never right after that

them Adams boys got a Mexican sheepherder
he can train the best sheepdog
of anybody round here they say
he takes the puppy way from the bitch
before his eyes gets opened up
lets him suck on a ewe
tied up to a fence till she dopts him
he grown up thinking he's a sheep
and hates whatall comes after them
but I dunno if I want a dog
that thought it was a sheep
might not even have sense
to lift its leg to piss on a tree
it goes both ways

some people back home
was so poor they eat rabbits
ever night for supper
so long their kids
would run under the porch
and hide ever time they heard
a dog bark
that's what they sed
but I wouldn't worry
about that boy of yours yet
he's still young
you got a couple years
to let it grow on you
where'd you say them steeples was?

Shoveling Rolled Barley

got this job selling trailerhouses
he couldn't do that neither
he'd run off all the customers
when they'd come on the lot
they'd look at this trailerhouse he'd say
you sure you can ford something like that?
mebbe you'd better go look at them one's
on the other side the lot
they more for people like you
it don't cost so much over there
you think it's enuf grain here
to fill up them other three self feeders?
it better be I cain't buy no more
so he went out this one time
set up this trailerhouse they'd solt
he was posta get it levelled
and this other guy he'd hook up the plumbing
Ellis Britton he didn't make no balance
in the middle he's just trying
to do it with the screwerup thingamajig
up on the tongue on the front
he's benting the trailerhouse frame
it wouldn't level
he'd screw it up and go look
the bubble would go one way
he'd go unscrew it back down and look
the bubble would be on the other end
he done it twice or three times

he got mad he taken his hammer
started beating on the front of the trailerhouse
looked like it'd been shot
with a cannonfull of ball bearings
all them little dents
that other guy who was there working
sez ohmygod Ellis Britton
what you doing?
Ellis Britton he sez
it isn't none of your goddam business
he thrown that hammer down
scrut it up again
but the bubble was off the other way
he set back and screamed
like he's a crazy womern
beat his hands up against the trailerhouse
till they was both bleeding like hell
sez goddam you goddam yousonofabitch
that's enuf in that one
let's pull the pickup over to the one
in that pen it's almost empty
he's so mad he went over got his torch
he lit it and burnt a hole in the end
of the trailerhouse he sez there by god
how'd you like that? so grapt
that screwerup turnt it up some more
bubble went to the other end
he had both ends of that trailerhouse
a foot up above the middle
it was all warped they never could fix it
his face went purple like a balloon
his eyes almost come out of the sockets
he picked up that torch
cut the tongue right off the trailerhouse
he hadn't put in no levelling blocks
up front that whole thing
come down right on the ground

busted all the winders out the doors
popped open they never could get them shut
he's so mad he cut that screwerup
in three pieces and thrown it over the fence
that other guy's just standing there
it wasn't nothing he could do but watch
it wasn't even no telephone to call his wife
he never sez nothing
with Ellis Britton holding that cutting torch
so when he's done
he flung the torch down he sez
that's it I quit
I cain't take this shit no more
he walked all the way back
to the trailerhouse lot by hisself
when he got there they already known
that other guy drove back and told them
what he'd done but he left
before Ellis Britton got there he sez I quit
pay me off right now
they give him his money too
they known what he might do
at night if they didn't
Ellis Britton he could hold up
his end of a grudge purdy good
help me back up to the feeder
don't let me knock it down
it isn't no sense to doing that
it wasn't nothing left for them to do
he'd ruint that trailerhouse for good
they figgered they come out ahead
if he'd just leave and not come back no more

August: Midnight Farrow

How beautifully brown
and deep
the red gilt's eyes
by lightning.

Hauling Hogs

FOR MY DAUGHTER
"How long till we get there?"

If I was to be a driver
forty years I'd never get used to it
or like it one bit
I cain't back up a trailer
worth a dam and I don't think
I'll ever get over worrying
about having a wreck
with all them hogs back there

that one truck that jackknifed
up on Black Ridge
they sed he was hauling
200 head of fat hogs to California
because of the train strike
it was pigs all over the freeway
about fifty of them dead
or had to be killed
some froze before they could get to them
I heard they only found
and got loaded about a hundred more
the rest run off in the bushes
when it split open barrows and gilts
I've drove up there twicet
to see if I could find them

what would you do John I sed
if you found them?

you couldn't catch them
they'd be too wild by now

I'd go home and load up
me a little boar and donate it
to the wild herd if I seen
any of them girl pigs running round
them barrows ain't doing them
any good they might as well
run off and live in San Francisco
I'd start a wild herd up there
get me a license to guide
or a brandingiron to catch strays

about ten years ago they say
more or less Walter Buckley
was bringing a load of cows
down off Cedar Mountain
he lost his brakes
come up on a State gravel truck
right on the U turn
it was a miracle he sed
he'd done told the Lord goodbye for now
be seeing you right soon
he rammed that gravel truck
from the back
they switched loads

gravel truck dumped
right on his cattle truck
mashed in the hood
busted his windshield out and
buried him up to his chest
in gravel running out
both side winders
them cows went right over the top
his truck into the bed

of the State truck
two of them hanging out the dump feed
four with broke legs
and half a dozen jumped out
run off into the forest
never found two of them
three on their backs bellering
that driver burnt his brakes
getting that truck stopped
about a yard from the clift edge
Walter Buckley sez
you got any matches? here's
some firewood by the road
I got a sharp knife
let's have a fry if you'll unbury me
he had three broke ribs and a arm
but he lived

I'd let you drive
but you ain't no bettern I am
like a monkey with a football
behind the steering wheel
look back there and see
what they doing
they jostling this truck
all over the road
tell them to be still
we almost there

September 1st

Winter's gone be here
before you known it sed John
I said yes, you can smell it in the air
can't you? but John sed no
I smoke I cain't smell nothing
but I can see
it's mice turds everwhar
you turn over a board or a lid
fifteen of them jump up and run
acrost your shoes
into the other room or
toward the house

LaVerne sez she done caught a dozen
in the traps and it's more
coming in I seen them
out the corner of my eye
in ever room and she sez
she can smell them
stinking up the house
like it ain't never been cleaned
and there's no cats left
Where'd they all go John I said
I haven't seen a cat in a month

if it wasn't against the law
I'd get me a shotgun
after that Robb boy

from down to Parowan or a board
whop his ast all the way home
he got that one lion dog
his daddy's the goverment trapper
so he trained it to hate cats
he taken it all over his town
turned it loose on ever cat he seen
let it kill it and then
drove him in his pickup
around Midvalley when it was a cat
he'd put that dog on it
even if it belonged to somebody else
and clumb up a tree after it
when it found one to throw him down
let that dog tear it up
Orella Lister had sixteen cats they say
which is too many
she needed them thinned
not all killed and she's only got
one left and it's one of them
Siamese twin cats that's cross-eyed
and been raised in the house
it ain't got sense to drink
out of a mud puddle
only thing it knows how to do
is wear a collar
and now look
it's mice everwhar

you cain't get rid of them
even if he hadn't killed your cat
I put a snake in the corn crib
when I's younger
until mama grapt it
by the neck and I haven't since
LaVerne has to set the traps
I cain't stand to do it

with my fingers all stiff
it ain't no way I can tell
when the spring's cocked
it goes off in my hand on my thumb
or just when I put it down
I holler and LaVerne gets mad
in the house so I say
if you don't like the noise
you do it she sez
get out of my way
I say why didn't you say so
in the first place then?
but I have to take the dead mice
out of the traps
she won't do that
they'd have to bury them right there

Why don't you get some poison,
John? I said
you can put that out
and let it do the work for you.
Oh shit, Roy Talbert did that oncet
he had mice all over his house
where he lived alone
never did get married
couldn't stand it finally
he took and bought some DeCon
four boxes of it I think
set it out
went off to work
he drove truck back then
was gone four days

when he got home he's hungry
made him a sandwitch
out of bananas and jelly
taken a bite and seen this mouse

laying dead on his floor
he walked through that house
looking to see forty-two mice
all dead while he's eating
his sandwitch and
it turnt his stomach he sed
he taken that DeCon
that was left outside
thrown it straight up in the air
as far as he could
and the rest of his sandwitch
he left and slept in a motel
for a week until the rest
of them mice was through dying
he couldn't take the thought
of it no more till it was over
he went home
scraped his floors with a grain shovel
to get whatall he could out
sed for a year he'd open
a drawer or a cubbordoor
it was a dead mouse looking at him
he wouldn't have no poison
in his house if you give it to him

I wisht we could get rid of them
or get them to stay away awhile
if we don't have two more weeks
of growing season
I'm gone have four bushel of chow chow
and no tomater juice
I ain't ready for winter yet
my garden ain't done
and it ain't even a cat to buy
around here now
him and that dog kilt them all
now look what happened

September

Evening:
the red sow
rises from her mud
to wade in
elm shadow.

Roofing the Barn

JOHN EDWARD LEFLER
MR 3 U.S. Navy
World War II
Feb. 19, 1917–Aug. 11, 1980

Splang bang bloing tooin
Hey, Norman, while you're down there
whyn't you take and get some more
of them leadheaded nails
I'm about out in my aporn
I got a few in my shirtpocket
LaVerne'll be calling us in
for suppertime pretty soon I bet
let's put four more pieces
of that eight foot sheetiron on now
before we quit to eat
on this part so it'll be done
sproing goddamit
I cain't get this one started
I wish they'd drilt starter holes
in it for you

Going to snow tonight John
I sed mebbe we ought not
to break for awhile longer
I can see that sed John
it's feathers coming down now
we got to hurry
if we can get this side done only
it's bettern nothing
I can crowd the sheep in over here
what about that barn
in Paragonah I heard almost burned down?

It didn't burn John,
the fire got to it but didn't
go up the side.
You wasn't there though to see?
No I sed I was out of town

We had a barn burner
back home oncet had everbody
wondering who it was setting fires
sed John Norman is that
goddam hammer down there somewhere?
What goddam hammer? sed Norman
that goddam two pound one
I can get these nails started with
sed John did you know
that feller got killed by the truck?
Yes I did John I sed
he was a friend of mine.
It's too bad about that
what was it happened?

It was a grass fire
in Ardell Talbert's backyard I sed
this the one you want? Norman sez
John sed thow it up here
that's the one
not so dam hard you gone
hit me in the mouth with it
so what then?
It spread across his backyard
I sed and ran toward
Wanda Benson's barn so they
sounded the alarm.
I know a man where I come from
sed Norman who burnt his barn down
over cats back home one time.
So how'd he get killed? sed John

He didn't but the cats did sed Norman
All the firemen jumped on the truck
he was in the front seat I sed
by the driver but jumped off
to get something and
somebody got his seat.
Lift me up one piece of sheetiron sed John
one of these? sed Norman
I got it I sed he wants eight footers
so he tried to get on the back
but slipped on the concrete
the truck went over him

This guy I know sed Norman
was name Clovis Bowen who was
milking cows in his barn
this one night with his boy there
I growed up with back then
named LeRoy Bowen
Here grab the end I sed
I got it sed John give it a push
For a long time they looked
all over to see who it was
setting them barns on fire back home
they thought mebbe it was somebody
for the insurance at first
but then it was too many
different ones so that couldn't be it
but it was all against Bryant Williamson's
insurance so they thought then
it was somebody out to get him
who's driving that truck
was it some kid?
It doesn't matter John
I sed it was an accident

John, LaVerne called from the house
supper's on the table.
We coming John yelled
soon as we get this one piece done
did it kill him right then?
No I sed it smashed his pelvis
but he never lost consciousness
he was mad and screaming at the kid
who stole his seat on the truck
They was cats sed Norman
up in the eaves and rafters
of Clovis's barn he screamed at
that caused his fire
this one cat that night must of set there
got hypmotised like they do
by the smell and the sound
of that squirt squirting in the bucket
of milk going in it
he fell over the edge
am I eating supper here or going home?
You eating here sed John
What we having then?
Probley some dam baloney sandwitch
she'll holler in a minute
it's getting cold if you don't come in

when'd they know they
run over him?
Not until later I sed
They knew that cat come down
right then sed Norman
I bet they did sed John
it took all summer of watching
to find who's setting them fires
then they caught him at it
it was Don Baker
one of Charley Baker's idiots

carrying matches they known
he's going round burning trashbarrels
he'd built his business up
to barns by then to watch them burn
didn't have nothing to do
with the insurance one bit
John LaVerne called you coming?

Directly we be right in
hand me up anothern
they put out the fire and never known
he wasn't even there?
They said Kevin stood on the hood
of the firetruck I sed
with his bullhorn yelling into it
"I have the authority to deputize
you on the spot."
Who bought him one of them? sed Norman
"I can arrest you if you refuse to help
fight this fire," he kept saying
That cat sed Norman come down
clawing holes in the air to hold on
Lift the side up so I can grab it
sed John right there I got it
He brung down a ½ bale of straw
a chicken's nest and four kittens
right on the cow's back

Chester Robertson I sed
was on the other side of the yard
telling the firemen where
to squirt their water
Did they listen to him? sed John
He's on the town council I sed
you bet they listened to him
half the town drove up
in their cars to watch

Nobody else was there that night
sed Norman except LeRoy
who his daddy had made stand up
holding the cow's tail
so he wouldn't be swatted in the face
when she tried to swoosh them flies
Don Baker was too much
of a idiot to keep flies off hisself
they couldn't do nothing to him
by law until he's eighteen years old
so he run off later sed John
almost burnt hisself up one time
hitched a ride on a truck
when he jumped off lit on his ast
he had his buttpocket filt with matches
they caught and got him on fire
but somebody seen it and put it out

splang JOHN
I told you I'm coming John sed
soon as I get this done right now
how'd they get the fire out
with that much help there?
Ardell's wife hooked up
a garden hose and did it I sed
Where's them nails I need? sed John
I'm done out by now
Here sed Norman I been standing here
holding them for you for a hour
since you asked me to
so that cow jumped straight up
and bellered so it scared LeRoy
he let go the tail and turned to run
she smacked Clovis in the eye
put cowshit in it where he couldn't see
jumped up him and LeRoy both
got their foot in the milkbucket

that cat screamed louder when he seen
Clovis cause he hated cats
clawed down the cow's side sliding off
kicked Clovis in the chest
right into where he'd just shoveled
fresh cowshit to get it
out of his way so he could milk
                    bam blam

Okay get anothern up here
before LaVerne has a brainspasm
hurry up now she's getting mad
so what happened to him?
It just knocked his wind out sed Norman
Here you go I said
it took a week for him to die.
Clovis was so mad
he got his gun to shoot that cat
but couldn't find it
They couldn't find Don Baker
sed John after that for a year
then brung him back from Texas
or Arkansas where the law had him
he went to work at his daddy's
junkyard till he's eighteen
they could put him in the state
insane asylum then they hoped
They's back in the rafters sed Norman
John this is the last time
I'm calling sed LaVerne
this food is getting cold
We coming I sed John sed

They was all meowing and squalling
he shot up a pocketful of shotgun shells
killed three chickens but no cats
Took him a week? John sed

He went into a coma
never came out of it
Well he never felt it that way
Don Baker was welting on a car
with a torch and cut
into the gas tank on it
blowed hisself all to hell
bet he got a bang out of that
When Clovis couldn't shoot them
he started hollering I'll get you
you sonofabitch I'll fix you
he went and burned his barn down
to get rid of them cats
Half the fire department I sed
didn't even go to his funeral
They didn't even have one for Don Baker
that I known of
that other sister of his
that her tongue hung out her mouth
they'd arredy tied her up insides
so she couldn't have no kids
after that carnival man
took her in the truck to show her
the snakes and knocked her up
but the baby died in her
they sed but others say
that wasn't what happened
they fixed her
when he heard about Don Baker
Dan Cockrum sed "there went
the town supply of idiots"
and Charlie Baker died of a heart attackt
somewhere about that time
The cow dried up sed Norman
she wouldn't be milked no more
I hope we finished now I'm hungry
I hope they ain't no more of them John sed

I hope he didn't feel it I thought
JOHN
   we coming I sed right NOW
let's go eat
      John sed
Lord bless this tunafish sandwitch
which we are about to receive
       a voice inside me breathed
Lord keep a strong roof
over all thy wayward sheep

Evening

No rest for the wicked
and the righteous don't need none

That's done up right and through
let's go have a coldbeer inside
and set on the furniture

No, John, I'm going home
I'm tired I'm going to bed
and I may not get up tomorrow
I may sleep all day

Oh no you cain't do that
the auction starts at nine
they do weinerpigs first
we got to be there

I'll call you early at six
so you can sleep till then
we gotta have breakfast
and go to the auction

so you take and go on home
I'll be by to get you
in my truck
             we got work to do
we gone buy us some pigs
make us some money
starting tomorrow morning

Coda

the dew lay all night upon my branch
JOB 29:19

John, are you sure you want
to buy these weiner pigs?
That's a lot of money.

Look, you want to go partners
or not? I done told you
I'll loan you the first half
don't you remember
the insurance sed it was
a act of god
now that means god must want
us to have these pigs
or he wouldn't of acted that way
you want to piss him off
you go ahead
but you tell him I done what
I thought he wanted me to
or he wouldn't of made me this way
is that what you want?

don't let me make up your mind
but LaVerne went to church
last Sunday they told a story
something about a man looking for a job
this tornado come up
blown off his house and crops
killed all his livestock
and his wife and family

cause they didn't have no storm cellar
they sed the Lord
he was mad at that man
I guess cause he didn't have no job

he got the hives
and mebbe the jockey strap itch all over
couldn't set still for scratching
here come the missionaries
to get him
it was three of them I imagine
a Mormon, a Jehovah Witness
and probley one of them Hairy Sutras
none of them made any sense
and then anothern come
probley a Camelite setting up
cottage meetings

he had enough
went back to church
and the Lord spoke in tongues
they grapt his head
hollered the words and healed him
found a widow woman with a family
for him and a farm on shares
as soon as he got his dues
paid up and the Lord
wasn't mad at him no more

Now I don't know
if that's a truestory or not
but do you want to take a chance
on it? I heard
the Lord gives and takes
this time he give
so I figger if we don't take
he ain't gone be pleased

and I don't have no storm cellar
and haven't got time to itch
do you?
so what you gone do about it
the auction starts in five minutes
you better make up your mind
right now

Pain

FOR WILLIAM KLOEFKORN

Now how'd you do that? sed John
and I told him
about the pickup being stuck
wouldn't start
how I got mad and put my back
against the front and started it rocking
then gave all I had
heard the discs rupture
even before I felt the blue pain
pick me up and throw me
on the ground
eyeball to antenna with a red ant
that crawled up my nose
and I didn't care

I've never hurt that way I said
it was the worst pain a man could feel

Oh shit sed John it is not
you lain back down right now
how'd you like it if I taken
and pult on these tractor ropes
they got you hooked up to
wouldn't that hurt just as bad
or worst?
and what if that one fat nurse
name Martha Rae come in
pull down your covers

with her crapper pan again
sez lift up you gotta try some more
staring at you and you ain't got
no underwears on?
you tell me that don't hurt some

and everbody comes in
sez well that ain't so bad
mine was worst
or my brother torn his back up
like yours and he still cain't walk
or he cain't stand up straight
or his pecker still don't have no feeling
in it and that was twenty years ago
or the doctor come in
sez we gone have to operate on you
and everbody you known
sed don't let him cut you
you'll be cripple for life
their uncle he's in a wheelchair
ever since cain't do nothing
slobbers down the front his shirt
nothing below his neck works
all the doctor's fault
you won't never be the same no more.
You gone tell me that ain't worst
to hear truestories like that
and you just laying on your butt
in the bed taking up space
from people that's really sick

No that ain't the worse
it ain't even the worse I heard of
I'll tell you about some pain

everybody knows about that feller
set down on a crapper

at Possom Kingdom Lake
got blackwidow spider bit
on his privates and the whole end of it
come off with the poison
but I known a man
had cancer in the mouth
hurt so bad he chewed
half his tongue off before he died
got blood poison and gangrene
anothern had to chop his leg off
with a hatchet to get out
of a beartrap or he'd froze to death
died anyway in a car wreck
going to his mother's funeral
a year later so it wasn't worth it
and old Dan Walker
when his tractor wouldn't start
hit it with a sledgehammer
missed and broke his shinbone
crawled a mile to his house
and they'd unhooked his phone
cause he's behind on the bill
that's pain

but theys some
that hurts a different way
sometimes even worst
it was this boy in the fifth grade
name George Mendietta
he would of stoled his daddy's pickup
given it to you
for this one little girl name Danella Hagins
to say hello to him
but he's a Mexican and that's too bad
for him back then
so he helt it in all year
here comes Valentine day

what'd he do? goes down
to Bob Collier drugstore
taken and bought her a box
of red Valentine candy and a card
given it to her at the class party
we all remembered
cause she cried and had to go
to the nurse's office
she's so embarrassed to have a Mexican
do such a thing to her
he never come back to school
the rest of the year
I think that hurt purdy good

that ain't the worse
I known of
I hurt just as bad
over Thelma Lou Shackleford
when I's seventeen
we all went out to eat fish
we'd been messing around all day
it was that night I known
I loved that girl moren life
we all order oysters and horse relish
cept Thelma Lou
she orders catfish and the man
sez you want that broil or fried maam?
she sez fried
I can still hear the way that sound
slid off the front of her tongue
I's so ashamed eating raw oysters
I couldn't hardly hold one
in my mouth and Tommy Wayne Clayborn
ate his and half of mine
slopped saucet all over the table
like a hog licking his fingers
I watched her eat ever bite

of her fish begging myself John
ask her to go for a ride
but I's too scared
afraid she might say no or laugh
when she's through
Tommy Wayne sez come on Thelma Lou
let's go up Sawmill Road
she never sed a word
got up and walked off with him
it wasn't nothing I could do
but watch her go

and that's not the worse
Thelma Lou was my sister's bestfriend
I known for a fact
cause Thelma Lou told her
she told me
how when she's twelve and come in
first time how she never known
what it was
nobody done told her
she thought she's busted something
bleeding to death
she went in the kitchen
told her mother
her mother never turnt around
sed you get out of this room
you shut the door behind you
cain't you see I'm cooking supper
I think that's worse

but even worst than that
was Tommy Wayne Clayborn
knocked her up and I think he done it
that night I couldn't say nothing
on the Sawmill Road
they didn't know what to do

everbody in town known about it
before they got around to telling their folks
finally Tommy Wayne told
his daddy name Shirley Clayborn
he's the sheriff back then and a good one
about the toughest man in town
partly because of his name
you'd say morning Shirley
he'd look right in your eye
if it was sparkling any
it wouldn't be purdy quick
so Tommy Wayne told him
he said what you gone do, boy?
Tommy Wayne sez gone marry her, daddy
Shirley sed is that what you want?
Tommy Wayne sez yas she's a hell of a girl
and she was goddammit
Shirley Clayborn called her family over
they all talked it out and sez okay
if that's how it is
nobody got his ast kicked
like he should of
when they left Tommy Wayne
was just standing there in the room
with his daddy
Shirley went over and poured
two glasses of bootleg whiskey
he'd confisgated out sez you want a drink?
Tommy Wayne sed yas I do I think
and they did
then Shirley Clayborn sez
boy, do you know what's worst
than doing what you did to that girl
in the back seat of my Chevrolet car?
and he sez no daddy, what?
Shirley Clayborn sed
not doing that to that girl

in the back seat of my Chevrolet

and that's pain.
All my life I've had to known
I never had a daddy like that
and it ain't no way I know how
to be one either
and you cain't tell me you hurt worst
than I do about that

and besides
I busted my back up
like yours
and I think mine's worst
when I got home
I couldn't set up in bed by myself
so LaVerne put a screw in the ceiling
we hooked up a comealong
to help me get up and a belt
round my chest
so I needed to pee and I hit that ratchet
belt slipped down round my belly
I done come along my back
up off the bed
I holler and here comes LaVerne
she don't know how to undo
that ratchet and let me down
she hit it three licks
there I am my head and feet
touching the bed and the rest of me
pretending to be a rainbow
with slipped discs
me needing to pee
the only way she could think of
to get me down so I'd quit hollering
was with a hacksaw
neighbors a mile off

heard me and come down fore
she got me cut loost
seen where I couldn't help it
peed all over my bed
I couldn't do nothing but
lay in it

so don't tell me about the worst pain
cause it ain't never the worse
it's always something bettern that
you can bet on it anyday
besides here come the fatnurse
so you better be getting ready, now.

David Lee is currently Chairman of the
Department of Language and Literature at
Southern Utah State College in Cedar City. He
has received several fellowships from the
National Endowment for the Humanities and
from the National Endowment for the Arts. His
publications include *The Porcine Legacy*
(Copper Canyon Press, 1978), *Driving and
Drinking* (Copper Canyon Press, 1979, 1982),
Shadow Weaver (Brooding Heron Press, 1984),
and *The Porcine Canticles* (Copper Canyon
Press, 1984). *Day's Work* was awarded the
Publication prize of the Utah Original Writing
Competition.

39092 00740952 9

SWEETWATER COUNTY LIBRARY SYSTEM
SWEETWATER COUNTY LIBRARY
GREEN RIVER, WY

DISCARD

SWEETWATER COUNTY LIBRARY
300 N. 1st E.
Green River, WY 82935
307-875-3615